LANCASHIRE
Wit & Humour

CAMILLA ZAJAC

BRADWELL
BOOKS

Published by Bradwell Books
9 Orgreave Close Sheffield S13 9NP
Email: books@bradwellbooks.co.uk

Complied by Camilla Zajac

British Library Cataloguing in Publication Data: a catalogue record for this
book is available
from the British Library.

1st Edition
ISBN: 9781902674605

Print: Gomer Press, Llandysul, Ceredigion SA44 4JL
Design by: JenksDesign
Illustrations: ©Tim O'Brien 2013

Two Lancastrians stop outside a shop window, one point's in and says 'Thar's t'one I'd get!' - so a Cyclops comes out and punches him.

Funny Lancashire place names:

Bottoms Fold

Tosside

Whambottom Lane

What gets wetter and wetter the more it dries?

A towel.

Bloke runs into a Salford pub:

'Anyone got a large black cat with a white collar?'

'No!'

'Drat! I've run over the Vicar...'

I never was, am always to be,
No one ever saw me, nor ever will,
And yet I am the confidence of all
To live and breathe on this terrestrial ball.
What am I?

Tomorrow.

The Beatles wrote a song about Wigan....

It's called Wigan work it out!

Harry proudly drove his new convertible into town and parked it on the main street, he was on his way to the recycle centre to get rid of an unwanted gift, a foot spa, which he left on the back seat.

He had walked half way down the street when he realised that he had left the top down... with the foot spa in the back.

He ran all the way back to his car, but it was too late...

Another five foot spas had been dumped in the car.

A little boy calls down to his mum from upstairs 'Mam! Maaaaa-am!'

'What's up, ewr Johnny?'

'Ewr Billy's tekin' all t' overcoat fer 'imsel'

(The Vicar has come to tea, the mother is embarrassed, and tries to make the best of things. She doesn't want the Vicar knowing she can't afford decent bedding...)

Silly lad! It's called an 'eiderdown', not an overcoat!

(A few minutes later)

A shout comes from upstairs - 'Mam! Maaaaa-am!'

What's up now, ewr Johnny?

'Ewr Billy's pull't'sleeve off our eiderdown!'

Did you hear about the two men from the monastery who opened up a seafood restaurant? One was the fish friar, and the other was the chip monk.

From the beginning of eternity

To the end of time and space

To the beginning of every end

And the end of every place.

What am I?

The letter 'e'.

Man walks into a butcher's shop on the Yorkshire side of the border. 'I'd like a pig's head please' The butcher calls in to the back 'One pig's head, Fred!' Then the customer says "Make that a Lancs pig's head' 'Take the brains out, Fred!'.

Did you hear that they've crossed a Newfoundland and a Basset Hound? The new breed is a Newfound Asset Hound, a dog for financial advisors.

All about, but cannot be seen.

Can be captured, cannot be held.

No throat, but can be heard.

What is it?

The wind.

What do you call a Mancunian in a filing cabinet?

Sorted!

Did you hear about the two men from the monastery who opened up a seafood restaurant? One was the fish friar, and the other was the chip monk.

I'm part of the bird that's not in the sky. I can swim in the ocean and yet remain dry. What am I?

A shadow.

Robert proudly drove his new VW Beetle convertible into town and had his shiny banjo nestling in the back seat.

He had walked half way around the block from the parked car when he realised that the sunny weather had caused him to leave the hood down... with his banjo in the back.

He ran all the way back to his car, but it was too late...

Another five banjos had been dumped in the car.

What goes around the world but stays in a corner?

A stamp.

During the War of the Roses, in a village near the border of Lancashire and Yorkshire, the villagers hear the cry "One Yorkshire man is stronger than one hundred Lancashire men."

The village is on the Lancashire side of the border. Offended, the angry villagers run towards the voice of the arrogant Yorkshireman, but none return.

The next day, in a village further along the border the same cry is heard. The villagers ran out to try to find the offensive Yorkshireman making such a bold claim, but again, no one returns to the village.

The next day, in another village on the Lancashire side of the border, the same cry is heard. But before the men of this village set off running, they are stopped by a lone survivor of the previous episodes. He runs towards them shouting 'Stop! Don't go! It's a trap! There's TWO of them!"

They say an Englishman laughs three times at a joke. The first time when everybody gets it, the second a week later when he thinks he gets it, the third time a month later when somebody explains it to him.

My life can be measured in hours;

I serve by being devoured.

Thin, I am quick; fat, I am slow.

Wind is my foe.

What am I?

A candle.

A group of chess enthusiasts checked into a hotel and were standing in reception discussing their recent tournament victories. After about an hour, the manager came out of the office and asked them to move. 'But why?' they asked, as they walked off. 'Because,' he said 'I can't stand chess nuts boasting in an open foyer.

An Englishman went into a hardware store and asked to buy a sink.

'Would you like one with a plug?' asked the assistant.

'Don't tell me they've gone electric,' said the Englishman.

A Preston man buys two horses and he can't tell them apart. So he asks the farmer who lives next door what he should do. The farmer suggests measuring them.

The Preston man comes back triumphantly and says: 'The white horse is two inches taller than the black horse!'.

Two boys were arguing when the teacher entered the room.

The teacher says, 'Why are you arguing?'

One boy answers, 'We found a ten pound note and decided to give it to whoever tells the biggest lie.

'You should be ashamed of yourselves,' said the teacher, 'When I was your age I didn't even know what a lie was.'

The boys gave the ten pound note to the teacher.

Six dozen dozen is greater than half a dozen dozen   yes or no?

No, both are equal.

A duck walks into a pub and goes up to the barman.

The barman says 'What can I get you?'

Duck: 'Umm. Do you have any grapes?'

Barman (Looking surprised):

'No, I'm afraid we don't.'

The duck waddles slowly out of the pub.

The next day at the same time, the duck waddles into the pub, hops up on a bar stool.

Barman: 'Hi. What can I get for you?'

Duck: 'Um. Do you have any grapes?'

Barman (a little annoyed): 'Hey! Weren't you in here yesterday. Look mate, we don't have any grapes. OK?'

The duck hops off the stool and waddles out of the door.

The next day, at the same time, the barman is cleaning some glasses when he hears a familiar voice

Duck: 'Umm... Do you have any grapes?'

The barman is really annoyed

Barman: 'Look. What's your problem? You came in here yesterday asking for grapes, I told you, we don't have any grapes! Next time I see your little ducktail waddle in here I'm going to nail those little webbed feet of yours to the floor. GOT me pal?'

So the duck hops off the bar stool and waddles out.

The next day at the same time, the duck waddles into the pub, walks up to the barman and the barman says,

'What on earth do YOU want?'

'Errrr. do you have any nails?'

'What!? Of course not.'

'Oh. Well, do you have any grapes?'

My bald uncle went to Lancashire.

Wigan?

No, he wore a hat.

I give you a group of three. One is sitting down and will never get up. The second eats as much as is given to him, yet is always hungry. The third goes away and never returns. What are they?

A stove, fire and smoke.

A man wanted to become a monk so he went to the monastery and talked to the head monk.

The head monk said, 'You must take a vow of silence and can only say two words every three years.'

The man agreed and after the first three years, the head monk came to him and said, 'What are your two words?'

'Food cold!' the man replied.

Three more years went by and the head monk came to him and said 'What are your two words?'

'Robe dirty!' the man exclaimed.

Three more years went by and the head monk came to him and said, 'What are your two words?'

'I quit!' said the man.

'Well', the head monk replied, 'I'm not surprised. You've done nothing but complain ever since you got here!'

A man enters a dark cabin. He has just one match with him. There is an oil lamp, a wood stove, and a fireplace in the cabin. What would he light first?

The match.

Though it is not an ox, it has horns; though it is not an ass, it has a pack-saddle; and wherever it goes it leaves silver behind. What is it?

A snail.

I went to a market in Lancashire last week.

Rawtenstall?

No, it was actually quite good.

When I am filled.

I can point the way:

When I am empty.

Nothing moves me.

I have two skins.

One without and one within.

What am I?

.evolg A

A customer ordered some coffee in a café. The waitress arrived with the coffee and placed it on the table. After a few moments, the customer called for the waitress 'Waitress,' he said, 'There's dirt in my coffee!', 'That's not surprising, sir', replied the waitress, 'It was ground only half an hour ago.'

You can have me but cannot hold me:

Gain me and quickly lose me.

If treated with care I can be great.

And if betrayed I will break.

What am I?

Trust.

An American photographer on holiday was inside a church in Leeds taking photographs when he noticed a golden telephone mounted on the wall with a sign that read '£10,000 per call'.

The American, being intrigued, asked a priest who was strolling by what the telephone was used for.

The priest replied that it was a direct line to heaven and that for £10,000 you could talk to God.

The American thanked the priest and went along his way.

Next stop was in Bradford

There, at a very large cathedral, he saw the another golden telephone with the same sign under it.

He wondered if this was the same offer as the one he saw in Leeds so he asked a nearby nun what its purpose was.

She told him that it was a direct line to heaven and that for £10,000 he could talk to God.

'OK, thank you,' said the American.

He then travelled to York, Scarborough, Keighley, Sheffield and Bridlington.

In every church he saw a golden telephone with the same '£10,000 per call' sign under it.

The American, upon leaving Yorkshire decided to travel to Lancashire to see if Lancastrians had the same phone.

He arrived in Burnley, and again, in the first church he entered, there was a golden telephone, but this time the sign under it read '50 pence per call.'

The American was surprised so he asked the priest about the sign. 'Father, I've travelled all over Yorkshire and I've seen a golden telephone in many churches. I'm told that it is a direct line to heaven, but in Yorkshire the price was £10,000 per call. Why is it so cheap here?'

The priest smiled and answered, 'You're in Lancashire now, son ... it's a local call.'

A new client had just come in to see a famous lawyer.

'Can you tell me how much you charge?', said the client.

'Of course', the lawyer replied, 'I charge £200 to answer three questions!'

'Well that's a bit steep, isn't it?'

'Yes it is,' said the lawyer, 'And what's your third question?'

Your mother's brother's only brother-in-law is your

Stepfather, Grandfather, Uncle or Father?

Your Father.

A passenger in a taxi tapped the driver on the shoulder to ask him something.

The driver screamed, lost control of the cab, nearly hit a bus, drove up over the curb and stopped just inches from a large plate glass window.

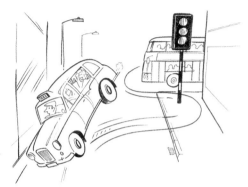

For a few moments everything was silent in the cab, then the driver said, 'Please, don't ever do that again. You scared the daylights out of me.'

The passenger, who was also frightened, apologised and said he didn't realize that a tap on the shoulder could frighten him so much, to which the driver replied, 'I'm sorry, it's really not your fault at all. Today is my first day driving a cab. I've been driving a hearse for the last 25 years.'

Local Police hunting the 'Knitting Needle Nutter' who has stabbed six people in Lancashire in the last 48 hours, believe the attacker could be following some kind of pattern.

My thunder comes before the lightning;

My lightning comes before the clouds;

My rain dries all the land it touches.

What am I?

A volcano.

What lies at the bottom of the ocean and twitches?

A nervous wreck.

What's the difference between roast beef and pea soup?

Anyone can roast beef.

I am so small, and sometimes I'm missed.

I get misplaced, misused, and help you when you list.

People usually pause when they see me,

So can you tell me what I could be?

A comma.

Why did the Lancastrian cross the road?

To defect to Edward IV.

What kind of ears does an engine have?

Engineers.

When one does not know what it is, then it is something; but when one knows what it is, then it is nothing?

A riddle.

He who has it doesn't tell it. He who takes it doesn't know it.
He who knows it doesn't want it. What is it?

Counterfeit money.

I went into the woods and got it. I sat down to seek it. I
brought it home with me because I couldn't find it. What is
it?

A splinter.

What can you catch but not throw?

A cold.

How many Lancastrians does it take to change a light bulb?

Seven. One to change the light bulb, one to pray with King Henry for the welfare of the new light bulb, two to bring the Duke of Suffolk and the Duke of Somerset their own light bulbs, two to hold Queen Margaret's train while she watches the bulb being changed, and one to stand against the door so the Duke of York doesn't find out.

I have holes in my top and bottom, my left and right and in the middle. What am I?

A sponge.

What kind of coat can only be put on when wet?

A coat of paint.

What goes round the house and in the house but never touches the house?

The sun.

A new client had just come in to see a famous lawyer.

'Can you tell me how much you charge?', said the client.

'Of course', the lawyer replied, 'I charge £200 to answer three questions!'

'Well that's a bit steep, isn't it?'

'Yes it is,' said the lawyer, 'And what's your third question?'

What goes round the house and in the house but never touches the house?

The sun.

A family from Wigan go on holiday to Benidorm and order some food. The father thinking his pie is lacking in gravy calls the waiter over saying ' 'ast tha Bisto fort pah?' and the waiter says in a southern English accent, 'I'm sorry, mate, I don't speak Spanish.'

A man walks into a doctor's office with two onions under his arms, a potato in his ear and a carrot up his nose. He asks the doctor: 'What's wrong with me?'

The doctor replies: 'You're not eating properly.'

What jumps when it walks and sits when it stands?

A kangaroo.

A Lancashire man fell out with his in-laws and banned them from entering the house while he was in it. The wife faithfully carried out his wishes until she was on her death bed and then asked sadly, 'I've always bin a good wife to thi, Jack?' 'Aye, lass; noan better,' he replied. 'Then I hope as 'ow you'll grant my last request and let our Mary Alice ride in th' first coach wi' thi at my funeral?' 'A'reet, lass,' he agreed heavily, 'But I'm warnin' thi, it'll spoil all mi pleasure!'

A man went on a trip on Friday, stayed for two days and returned on Friday. How is that possible?

Friday is a horse!

The leader of a large vegetarian society just couldn't control himself any more. He just needed to try some pork, just to see what it tasted like. So one summer day he told his members he was going away for a break. He left town and headed to the nearest restaurant. After sitting down, he ordered a roasted pig, and impatiently waited for his delicacy. After just a few minutes, he heard someone call his name, and to his horror he saw one of his fellow members walking towards him. Just at that same moment, the waiter walked over, with a huge platter, holding a full roasted pig with an apple in its mouth. 'Isn't that something,' says the man after only a moment's pause, 'All I do is order an apple, and look what it comes with!'

Who succeeded the first Prime Minister?

The second one!

What's a Wigan kebab?

Three pies on a stick.

What time does Sean Connery arrive at Wimbledon?

Tennish.

What, when you need it you throw it away, but when you don't need it you take it back?

An anchor.

A man goes into a pub in Blackburn and says 'A pie and a pint of beer'.

Landlord says 'Whitbread?' Man says 'Aye...five slices'.

A man went into a shop in Burnley and asked the owner if he sold 'Turps'.

The owner asked 'Would that be cassette turps or video turps?'

You can have me but cannot hold me;

Gain me and quickly lose me.

If treated with care I can be great.

And if betrayed I will break.

What am I?

Trust.

A Wiganer is walking through the desert when he stumbles across an old lamp. He picks it up and rubs it and a genie appears before his eyes.

'You have two wishes,' the genie says 'Use them wisely.'

So the Wiganer says 'I want an everlasting pie!'

So the genie gives him the pie. The Wiganer eats a bit of it then says 'Mmm that's good. Second wish - I want another one of these'.

"Brothers and sisters have I none, yet that man's father is my father's son" who is "that man"?

That man is your son.

38

A man is rushing to a hospital from a business trip because his wife has just gone into labour with twins, and there is a family tradition that the first family member to arrive gets to name the children. The man is afraid his wayward brother will show up first and give his kids horrible names. When he finally arrives at the hospital in a cold sweat he sees his brother sitting in the waiting room, waving, with a silly grin on his face. He walks unhappily in to see his wife who is scowling and holding two little babies, a boy and a girl. Almost afraid to hear it, the man asks, 'What did he name the girl?' 'Denise' says the wife. 'Hey that's not too bad! What did he name the boy?' 'De-nephew.'

What is it that you can keep after giving it to someone else?

Your word

What's the difference between an old bra and Wigan Athletic?

One has no cups and little support and the other can be found in a bin outside M&S.

What do you get if you cross a nun and a chicken?

A pecking order!

The more you take, the more you leave behind.

What are they?

Footsteps.

Two little girls wur walkin' down't'road carryin a baskit and cryin' their eyes up, an they cum across an owd man....

'Ayup mester, can yer 'elp us, us cat's badly'

Man - 'Ayup me ode ducks, wots up wi' it? ay it a tom?'

Girls - 'Naw ya daft one, it's in t' baskit'.

Did you hear about the man who was convicted of stealing luggage from the airport?

He asked for twenty other cases to be taken into account.

What comes once in a minute, twice in a moment, but never in a thousand years?

The letter M.

Language student to teacher, 'Are 'trousers' singular or plural?'

Teacher, 'They're singular on top and plural on the bottom.'

Why was the computer so tired when it got home?

Because it had a hard drive!

What do you get when you cross a dog with a telephone?

A Golden Receiver!

What walks all day on its head?

A nail in a horse shoe.

How many Man United fans does it take to change a light bulb?

560,001. That is: 1 to change it, 60,000 to say they've been changing it for years and 500,000 to buy the replica kit.

What did the cheese salesman say?

'That cheese may be Gouda, but this one is Feta!'

A box without hinges, key, or lid. Yet golden treasure inside is hid. What is it?

An egg.

What do you give a sick budgie?

Tweetment.

There are many good things to come out of Yorkshire - most of them roads into Lancashire.

I am seen in places that appear to need me not.

I come seldom to places that need me most.

Sometimes my arrival is celebrated.

at others times I am hated.

I refresh all things whether they need it or not.

Rain.

Bloke runs into a Salford pub, bleeding profusely:

'Whose is that black Jaguar on the car park?'

Light as a feather.

Nothing in it.

Few can hold it.

For even a minute.

Your breath.

46

What gear were you in at the moment of the impact?

Gucci sweats and Reeboks.

What's green and runs around the garden?

A hedge.

How do you know if you're a pirate or not?.

You just know you arrrrrhh.

What always ends everything?

The letter 'g'.

Two blokes go into t'pub.

Pint o'bitter, and a half o'shandy for my mate 'Donkey', please!

'Ere - what's with him calling you 'Donkey'?

Oh, 'e aw, 'e aw, 'e allus calls me that!

How many cats are in a small room if in each of the four corners a cat is sitting, and opposite each cat there sit three cats, and at each cat's tail a cat is sitting?

Four cats - each near the tail of the cat in the adjacent corner (it's a small room!)

Missus! Tha' dog's spoilt!

How dare you, sir!

No, it's spoilt - I ran over it wi' mi' truck...

How do you make a sausage roll?

Push it!

What was given to you, belongs to you exclusively and yet is used more by your friends than by yourself?

Your name.

Why is 6 afraid of 7?

Because 7, 8, 9!

Two snowmen are standing in a field. One says to the other 'That's funny, I can smell carrots.'

Why do seagulls live by the sea?

Because if they lived by the bay they would be called bagels.

A man was letting his dog run on Blackpool beach when it led him across to a man buried up to his head in the sand, hoarsely calling for help....

He ran up and asked the guy what had happened...The man said that some yobs had buried him for fun and he was so scared the tide would come in and drown him.

'Don't worry', said the first man, (as his dog licked the guy's face) 'I'll quickly go to get my ice shovel from my parked car and dig you out'.

'Is it a big one?' asked the partially buried guy...

'Why do you ask?' said the dog owner...

'Well, you're going to need a big shovel.... I'm sitting on a donkey!'.

How many surrealists does it take to screw in a lightbulb?

Banana.

What does one star say to another star when they meet?

Glad to meteor!

An Englishman, an Irishman and a Scotsman walk into a bar.

The Barman says 'Is this a joke?'

A girl who was just learning to drive went down a one-way street in the wrong direction, but didn't break the law. How come?

.gniklaw saw ehS

Two aerials meet on a roof - fall in love - get married. The ceremony was rubbish - but the reception was brilliant.

What do you do if you are driving your car in Manchester and you see a spaceman?

Park in it, of course.

What do the donkeys at Blackpool beach get for lunch?

Half an hour! Ye whit?

I do not breathe, but I run and jump.

I do not eat, but I swim and stretch.

I do not drink, but I sleep and stand.

I do not think, but I grow and play.

I do not see, but you see me every day.

I am a leg.

Where do generals keep their armies?

Up their sleevies.

Did you hear about the Lancashire lorry driver who was seen desperately chiselling away at the brickwork after his lorry got stuck while passing through a tunnel?

'Why don't you let the air in your tyres down a little?' asked a friendly passer by.

'Nay love,' replied the man 'It's t'roof that won't go under, not t'wheels'.

A man builds a house rectangular in shape. All the sides have southern exposure. A big bear walks by. What colour is the bear? Why?

The bear is white because the house is built on the North Pole.

What is the longest word in the English language?

Smiles. Because there is a mile between its first and last letters.

Why couldn't Cinderella be a good soccer player?

She lost her shoe, she ran away from the ball, and her coach was a pumpkin.

The old king is dying, and wants to leave his kingdom to the wiser of his two sons. He tells them that he will hold a horse-race, and the son whose horse is the last to reach the bridge and come back will inherit the realm. Immediately the younger son jumps on a horse and makes for the bridge at top speed. The king now knows that this is the wiser son, and leaves him the kingdom. Why?

The younger son jumped on the older son's horse. He realized that if they rode their own horses the race would never end.

A Lancashire man shouts urgently into the phone, 'My wife is pregnant, and her contractions are only two minutes apart!'

'Is this her first child?' the Doctor queries.

'No you idiot!' the man shouts. 'This is her husband!'

If it's not the day after Monday or the day before Thursday, and it isn't Sunday tomorrow, and it wasn't Sunday yesterday, and the day after tomorrow isn't Saturday, and the day before yesterday wasn't Wednesday, what day is it?

Sunday.

Two people are in a Lancashire butchers shop and one of them says `I bet you £100 that you can't reach that piece of meat on the ceiling and the other man says 'I'm not betting!'. The first man says 'Why not?' and the other man says `The steaks are too high!'

What is it that never asks you any questions and yet you answer?

Your phone.

What do cats like to eat for breakfast?

Mice Krispies

A farmer was driving along a Lancashire country road with a large load of fertiliser. A little boy, playing in front of his house, saw him and called, 'What do you have in your truck?'

'Fertiliser,' the farmer replied.

'What are you going to do with it?' asked the little boy.

'Put it on strawberries,' answered the farmer.

'You ought to live here,' the little boy advised him. 'We put sugar and cream on ours.'

What has a head like a cat, feet like a cat, a tail like a cat, but isn't a cat?

A kitten.

A farmer and his pig were driving down the road in rural Lancashire when a policeman pulled him over. The policeman asked the farmer, 'Didn't you know it's against the law to ride with a pig in the front of your tractor?'

The farmer replied, 'No, I didn't know that.' The policeman asked the farmer where he was going and he said, 'To Chipping'.

The policeman said, 'I will let you off the hook this time if you promise to take the pig to a farm when you get to Chipping.' So the farmer promised he would.

Several days later the policeman spotted the farmer with the pig driving down the road and pulled him over again. He said 'I thought I told you to take this pig to a farm when you got to Chipping.'

The farmer replied, 'I did and we had so much fun, I'm taking him to a fair next'.

Pete and Larry hadn't seen each other in many years. They were having a long chat to fill in the gaps by telling each other about their lives. Finally Pete invited Larry to visit him in his new apartment in Manchester. 'I have a wife and three kids and I'd love to have you visit us.'

'Great. Where do you live?'

'Here's the address. There's plenty of parking behind the flat. Park and come around to the front door, kick it open with your foot, go to the lift and press the button with your left elbow, then enter! When you reach the sixth floor, go down the hall until you see my name on the door. Then press the doorbell with your right elbow and I'll let you in.'

'Great. But tell me...what is all this business of kicking the front door open, then pressing lift buttons with my right, then my left elbow?'

Pete answered, "Surely you're not coming empty-handed?'

A strong young man working on a busy Manchester construction site was bragging that he could outdo anyone in a feat of strength. He made a special case of making fun of Morris, one of the older workmen. After several minutes, Morris had had enough.

'Why don't you put your money where your mouth is?' he said. 'I will bet a week's wages that I can haul something in a wheelbarrow over to that outbuilding that you won't be able to wheel back.'

'You're on, old man,' the boaster replied. 'It's a bet! Let's see what you got.'

Morris reached out and grabbed the wheelbarrow by the handles. Then, nodding to the young man, he said, 'All right. Get in.'

What do you call a boomerang that won't come back?

A stick.

A Lancashire man is in bed with his wife when there is an unexpected knock on the door. He rolls over and looks at his clock, and it's half past three in the morning. 'I'm not getting out of bed at this time,' he thinks, and rolls over.

A louder knock follows. 'Aren't you going to answer that?' says his wife.

So the man drags himself out of bed and goes downstairs. He opens the door and there is strange man standing at the door. It didn't take the homeowner long to realise the man was drunk.

'Hi there,' slurs the stranger. 'Can you give me a push?'

"No, I'm sorry It's half past three. I was in bed,' says the man and he slams the door. He goes back up to bed and tells his wife what happened.

'That wasn't very nice of you,' she says.

'Remember that night we broke down in the pouring rain on the way to pick the kids up from the babysitter, and you had to knock on that man's house to get us started again? What would have happened if he'd told us to get lost?'

'But the guy was drunk,' says the husband.

'Well we can at least help move his car somewhere safe and sort him out a taxi,' says the wife. 'He needs our help.' So the husband gets out of bed again, gets dressed, and goes downstairs. He opens the door, and not being able to see the stranger anywhere, he shouts, 'Hey, do you still want a push?' And he hears a voice cry out, 'Yes please!' So, still being unable to see the stranger, he shouts,

'Where are you?'

'I'm over here,' the stranger replies, 'on your swing.'

Sam, a Lancashire office professional, walks into his boss's office. He says 'I'll be honest with you, I know the economy isn't great, but I have three companies after me, and I would like to respectfully ask for a pay rise.'

After a few minutes of haggling his manager finally agrees to a 5% raise, and Sam happily gets up to leave.

'By the way', asks the boss as Sam is getting up, 'Which three companies are after you?'

'The electric company, the water company, and the phone company', Sam replies.

What has five eyes, but cannot see?

The Mississippi River.

A life-long city man, tired of the rat race in his home town of Preston, decided he was going to give up the city life, move to the country, and become a chicken farmer. He bought a nice organic chicken farm in a rural part of Lancashire and moved in. It turned out that his next door neighbour was also a chicken farmer. The neighbour came for a visit one day and said, 'Chicken farming isn't easy. So, to help you get started, I'll give you 100 chickens.'

The new chicken farmer was delighted. Two weeks later the neighbour dropped by to see how things were going. The new farmer said, 'Not too well mate. All 100 chickens died.' The neighbour said, 'Oh, I can't believe that. I've never had any trouble with my chickens. I'll give you 100 more.' Another two weeks went by and the neighbour dropped in again. The new farmer said, 'You're not going to believe this, but the second 100 chickens died too.' Astounded, the neighbour asked, 'What went wrong?'

The new farmer said, 'Well, I'm not sure whether I'm planting them too deep or too close together.'

Why do Northerners prefer mushy peas?

Because they can't keep the round ones on their knives.

What type of cheese is made backwards?

Edam.

What starts with a 'P', ends with an 'E' and has thousands of letters?

The Post Office!

A General inspecting troops in Hampshire ordered the parade to put on gas masks. He paused opposite a Lancashire soldier. Pointing to the eyepiece of his respirator, he inquired: 'Soldier, where is your anti-mist?' 'Don't know, Sir' came the reply 'Think she's oop with Uncle Albert in Oldham'.

A Lancashire man's dog dies and as it was a favourite pet he decides to have a gold statue made by a jeweller to remember the dog by.

Lancashire man: "Can tha mek us a gold statue of yon dog?"

Jeweller: "Do you want it 18 carat?"

Lancashire man: "No I want it chewin' a bone yer daft man!"

When is a yellow dog most likely to enter a house?

When the door is open.

At a pub in Lancashire town, a newcomer asks a Lancashire man ....
'Have you lived here all your life?'

After a long pause the man replies 'Don't know yet!'

What five letter word can have its last four letters removed and still sound the same?

QUEUE - remove "UEUE", say Q. Q and queue are pronounced the same.

Funny Lancashire phrases

Thaz a face lahk a constipated bloodhound!

(Smile, please.)

Th'art purrin' (putting thi yed in a dog kennel!)

(Don't mess about with me or you'll get in trouble.)

Th'art nor 'avvin' me on a butty.

(Don't try it on with me.)

Art tawkin' ter me or chewin' a brick?

(You are conversing rather indistinctly.)

Thammun gerrit thisen.

(You must get it yourself.)

Initot?

(Isn/t it hot?)

Gerritetten.

(Get it eaten.)

Supitup.

(Drink it up.)

You know you're a northerner when ...

You know the four seasons - winter, still winter, not winter and almost winter.

You know you're a northerner when ...

Driving in winter is better, because all the potholes get filled with snow.

What do you call a hippie's wife?

Mississippi.

What did Geronimo shout when he jumped out of the aeroplane?

ME!

You know you're a northerner when ...

You feel warm and toasty at minus 26.

You know you're a northerner when...

You find minus 40 a mite chilly.

You know you're a northerner when...

Your dog wears boots too.

You know you're a northerner when...

The mayor greets you on the street by your first name.

You know you're a northerner when...

If you don't go out for lunch you miss the sunrise and sunset.